PARTWAY TO GEOPHANY

PARTWAY TO GEOPHANY

{ poems }

~~Brendan Galvin~~

For Karen + Andy from Uncle Brendan All the Best!

Louisiana State University Press

Baton Rouge

Published by Louisiana State University Press
www.lsupress.org

Designer: Laura Roubique Gleason
Typefaces: MillerText, text; ITC Bookman BT, display

Cover photograph by Brendan Galvin

Thanks to the editors of the following magazines for publishing many
of these poems, some in earlier versions: *Cincinnati Review, Cortland
Review, Crab Orchard Review, Crazyhorse, Cutbank, Epoch, Georgia
Review, Gettysburg Review, Greensboro Review, Harvard Review,
Hudson Review, Ibbetson Street, Laurel Review, Mississippi Review, New
Hibernia Review, Northern Woodlands, Quarterly West, Sewanee Review,
Shenandoah, Southern Review, Tar River Poetry,* and *Terrain.*

Library of Congress Cataloging-in-Publication Data

Names: Galvin, Brendan, author.
Title: Partway to geophany : poems / Brendan Galvin.
Description: Baton Rouge : Louisiana State University Press, [2020]
Identifiers: LCCN 2020010655 (print) | LCCN 2020010656 (ebook) |
    ISBN 978-0-8071-7221-6 (paperback) | ISBN 978-0-8071-7453-1 (pdf)
    | ISBN 978-0-8071-7454-8 (epub)
Subjects: LCGFT: Poetry.
Classification: LCC PS3557.A44 P37 2020 (print) | LCC PS3557.A44
    (ebook) | DDC 811/.54—dc23
LC record available at https://lccn.loc.gov/2020010655
LC ebook record available at https://lccn.loc.gov/2020010656

For JC, jazz singer on Rush Street,
Chicago, and other venues, Off-Broadway actor,
fiction writer, essayist, poet,
in Loving Memory

Geophany: language that engages in "a secular celebration of the Earth, with the height and power of the religious tradition but purged of supernaturalism."

—Tim Robinson, *Dublin Review*

CONTENTS

PARTWAY TO GEOPHANY

I

Trance

After the downy woodpecker
not much bigger than a salt shaker
landed on your knee and looked
into your face, how long did it last?
Contemplating each other on the porch
where you sat, as though you had
gone so deeply into yourself
that you or something else
had summoned the bird to bring
you back, did it know
what your need was, that look
a blessing intense enough
to acknowledge all the songs
you have given this world, or
the proud mother you are,
or was that bird another version
of a child who wished to honor
the safe house for women
and kids you kept, or else
that mule deer you exchanged
gazes with one summer day
on a Black Hills path? If it were
me, the man who made you
this poem, I would have kissed
your knee before I flew.

February Light

Now the sun begins
greening up the amaryllis's
long but harmless blades
so it looks close to popping
a red flower in the bay window.
Afternoons the woodstove
seems less hungry,
but the difference this year
is you coming down the walk
through this light, improving it.
Emailing each other
at the same moment so often
had almost convinced me
we were meant for one another,
my darling, it was someone's
intention for us, or something's,
but we finalized it
that night you bespoke me
from your sleep with "What's
the Greek word for *Death*?" Sure
we talk to each other in the dark,
and rub our stories together,
your voice like a new flavor
of ice cream, but that night
sleep must have cleared my mind
entirely and I told you *Thanatos*,
proof we belong side by side
in one bed forever.

A Half-Moon in March

It isn't the shoulder zings or clicking knee
or orthotics in my shoes, not even because
yesterday I couldn't remember *shade,*
so wrote "pick up two lamp hats."
I will not see you tonight but wish I did.
It was after reading your poems
and realizing that a white-headed man
can wave at the moon too. My white head
is full of ballads I picked up in high school
before I went out for football, and now
they are full of your name, only yours.
As I listen to the owls and watch the shed
I shingled in a spryer year
absorb its nightly darkness, it seems that the owls
are asking for you, as I am, and had also
missed you singing "La Vie L'amour" on Rush St.
We are so much closer now, you and I and the owls,
but what I need tonight is your palm on
the back of my neck, and your voice in my ear
saying something to melt my kneecaps.
If I could gaff-rig my double-ender
to that half-moon up there
I'd be at your door in half an hour.

Summer Dawn, Summer Nightgown

I love the way light travels these mornings,
and the way you leave shades and windows open
so at four or five a.m. it assures our waking
to pines and a tidal wave of birdsong
rising from the east, music we know
or don't know, robin and cardinal, sure,
but also that one you call the narcissist warbler,
see me see me, or the teakettle bird
and the one offering *free beer,*
some others just passing through,
and the sadness of mourning doves
washing over our roof as we laugh and talk,
at our age as intricately twined as though
we are life's final gift to each other,
until you rise in your summer nightgown's
revelations, and flow to the dresser,
and flip that two-euro coin you brought
from Donegal, to decide who will make the coffee.

You, and the *Ursus* Remembered

When you said you wished a ferry
ran between Montauk and Truro,
I remembered the *Ursus*
Jim Surrey and I built forty years ago.
Writing all morning, the afternoons
given to sawing and planing, driving pegs
with mallets, by September our carpentry
had the shape of those double-enders
that carry drinking water among
the Greek isles, its beam the width
of a Block Island Cowhorn's.

Jim and the *Ursus* have sailed only God
knows where, Love, and each year
about this time a change of air proves
bittersweet at best, but if it anchored now
in Pamet Harbor, I'd sail for
Block Island today, then for you
and Montauk, and bring you here
for the nightly owl network and the morning
Corn Hill walk with me, then the sun
on our bedroom deck while I whistle
two redtail hawks into a circle
above our heads, or perhaps
bet on a chipmunk race.

Or lie in bed tonight hearing
the rain talk and telling each other a few
things we know: I'd open one eye
and look at you slyly as I said,
quoting Santayana, "To feel beauty
is a better thing than to understand
how we come to it."

Then you'd reply how you learned
that condors can sometimes fly
as high as jets, like 30,000 feet,
and I would ask if you knew that
a shooting star is a flying rock,
and you would say Basho said "A poet
becomes the thing observed and enters into it."
With that coming at me like a bullet of joy,
I would say, "You flip my pancakes every morning."

Paired in Time

1.
Let's take to our deck chairs
while we can, and watch
the year come apart as all
years have and will:
the marsh releasing seeds
in floaters and silky stars
rising and falling through the air
lighter than mosquitoes and
uncatchable in our palms,
as if we could impede
their progress anyway. Above,
on the edge of that
autumnal cloud, a single mote,
a raptor hanging like
a hauled anchor, one more
emblem of departure, though
at that height who could say
which kind of hawk? And still
farther above it all,
the occasional silver jet streak.
Whoever can say how deep
that blue is above everything
can also count the number
of Saturday lovers flying into
Logan today, and all
who have met the way we have,
by grace or luck paired in time.

2.
Consider the three hundred million things
against our ever happening into the Thing
we are, like how far Clearview, Iowa,
is from here, and what an elegant

high school majorette you must have been
in your white boots, Muse, while I was
spraying liquid asphalt on the back roads
of Massachusetts. Poetry makes nothing
happen? Your poems and mine
made us happen, after you found me
and phoned to say of a garden
I planted in a quarterly
that you'd never look at a toad
in the same way again. Was it chance
on a fall evening coming home from Ciro's
that you would sing me Édith Piaf
in your perfect French? Are our common
Donegal origins chance? Because
I would appear at age 77 in your mailbox,
on the cover of your daughter's
alumni magazine, I no longer believe in chance.

Where's My Gadabout Girl Tonight?

Sturgis? Talkeetna? A stage Off Broadway
or in L.A., a jazz club in Chicago?
There must be more than a few
drops of Tinker blood in you,
my Donegal darling. You are one
of the Traveling People and even the stray
animals know it. That's why a cormorant
waited before stepping off to strut
the white line in front of your bumper,
and the village animal officer shows up
each time you phone-in a vagrant
porcine mutt you've shoved onto
your back seat. The yard cat you lure
with a full bowl each evening,
even that mule deer you met eye-to-eye
in a dry creek bed knew it. Whichever way
they are headed, you toe-nudge
the turtles to roadside. By your stairs
the nightly possum awaited your return,
but if all your vagabonding gave you
the nerve to sit under a bookstore table,
reading, why did I have to take you
into the beech forest with sunflower seeds
to cure your fear of chickadees and titmice?

Hrafn

A two-footer on the skylight, hammering.
Raven, you're the first I've seen since climbing
the Isle of Lewis to the Callanish Stones circle,
and may be the first in these woods
since the Puritans departed. Before now,
only a few sizeable crows here that stuck
around Rock Harbor, Pamet, and Corn Hill.

Hrafn as I read in Old Norse, long before
seeing one. Did you use some ancient lore,
some proverbial good or evil, to fly from
your black silhouette on a Viking banner
into our third dimension, or merely slide
down the snowed roofs of Kobuk, or
lift off your roost on a DEW Line girder
or the Tower of London? Cleverest
and hoarsest of birds, what brought you
to my roof to give off ominous *prruuucks*?

Your kind is on the walls of Lascaux,
and fed Elijah, and in Egypt was a promise
of long life. Two there stood for monogamy,
but elsewhere a ravenstone meant beheadings.
Forget your groaning this evening. Utter
a short sentence to tell me if my namesake saint
is sailing for the Vestmanna Isles again,
or if my beloved has departed for God.

There Are Times I Need to Forget You

On this ladder, under the sped-up clouds,
for instance, when a week's weather's
spun and dispersed in an hour,
and I've been fighting nudges at the edge
of concentration, recalling the way
you used to look on the banks of the river
in your black one-piece swimsuit.

I adored you from your smallest toes
to your longest hair, and the parts
between. But forgive me, I need to forget you
up here where paint's blistered dry
as the papery nests of hornets,
and caulking peels off in shoelace lengths.

In the three years I needed you most
you sang to me in your Off-Broadway
phrasing, "You're my guy, it's time you knew,
all I am belongs to you," and I returned,
"I love you, Savannah's mother, and my love
is true. Remember, Savannah's mother,
I'm a one-girl guy." Or words to that effect,
not Off Broadway, just off.

Not true but generous, you claimed I had
a voice, even as the world was drifting away
that had given you venues on Rush St.
and at posh hotel lounges. Now you are under
midwestern snow. If I keep wishing
you were gripping the lower rungs

while I'm up here drawing a bead on seams
in corners where snow will build
and stay on inventing shades of blue,
snow will find its way in.

II

Ryders Cove

Shreds of nonsequitur, clipped
phrases and scribbles
clumped like compost, then stirred up
and returned to in a week. The usual
pre-poem mud: at times
no way of telling vowel
from consonant, but hoping for clues,
accretions, until the return of calendars,
proxies, signatures, panics of
subtraction that bury the notebook.

But driving down route 28 this morning
an osprey ripped me from lawyers
and pigeonholes as surely as if
it had plucked me off the water.
It flew above Ryders Cove
with a rag of tarp or plastic lifted
off a workboat's deck and borne
like a trailing banner through the air,
toward the skyward tip of a rusty pylon,
where its mate tucked and worried at
the impressive fright wig
of their nest under construction.

I said it out loud—*Excelsior!*—
and at home began to draw arrows
across the page, connecting
a few tendrils that appeared
out of the heap, circling
and underlining, nudging whatever
wanted to grow there toward
the promise of several hours
exempt from gravity.

One Willet

No piping plovers nesting in the dunes
this spring, but a willet cruises me
every morning on my way to the jetty,
repeating its name so I don't forget it,
or take it for a whimbrel. I know the black-
and-white wing stripes a willet raises
to warn off predators like me or attract
a mate, and I know the curve of
a whimbrel's beak from this thick
straight one and how it plucks fiddler crabs
from the mudflats, which once earned
willets the name "humility." I know its
downcurve of wings and the nervous
flight that betrays a nest in this saltmarsh,
though I do not want to know where.
Those wing feathers never graced
a woman's hat or hair the way
a great egret's or many a shorebird's did,
nor did the willet's breast often grace
a dinner table. This one has sailed
as if from the 19th century, as if escaped
from birdshot and men who posed behind
dead mounds of feathers and brought
the vaunted nest eggs to the kitchen. As if
it knew enough not to circle back, calling
to the fallen of its flock.

Winter Warbler

When the north wind blew it
like a fireworks of feathers
at the windows and past the hanging suet
and seeds, I never saw any owl
or merlin, it was over that quickly,
and I hoped the victim wasn't
a yellow-rumped warbler
as the blown colors hinted—
blue gray, black and white, a touch
of lemon. First thing the following morning
I put out the feeders I retrieve
against raccoons before each sunset,
and faster than coffee can brew
the complete bird was there,
batting cleanup for crumbs on the railing,
the only warbler that winters on this coast,
surviving on bayberries, waiting around for
weevils, borers, maggots, grubs, sawflies,
things that make holes in other things.

Best March Breakfast

Because an icicle thick as
a pro-tackle's forearm
has hung out there
for fifty winters, and a nuthatch
yesterday clutched it, sipping
the dripmelt, and after sunset
a shadow tiptoed across the deck,
coyote, to sit like something
out of Aesop beneath
the suet cage, and wish,
I am not hoping for the day
when butterflies turn
into money, or even the minute
when a brown clench
on the other side of this glass
unfists a spider turned in
on a grudge larger than
any headsman's axe,
especially because this
morning the ground's
in motion—a flock of bobwhites
foraging, their backs like
pine duff. In only forty
cubic feet, three illustrations
in twenty-four hours of life
wanting to be life.

One Answer

When will I be like the swallow?
—Pervirgilium Veneris

You will be like the swallow when
you stop noticing the pine warbler's
lunula, and the fiddleheads
risen and gossiping together
like a tribe of African meerkats.

It could mean turning a deaf ear
to imperfection, to that robin singing
like a rusty whip-poor-will
from a promontory branch,

its livery wasted on these dusks,
its broken thrush music seeming to draw
starbursts out of the sleeping trees,
red dwarfs from the maples,
the constellated petals of wild apple.

It could signal an end to nights of rain
when the earth softens and swells so
you feel it and wonder how anyone
anywhere ever thought it was flat.

You remember eyes that glittered
like ice flowers on a lapel
when you were seven or eight,
the way her perfume began to overrule
the cold and blend with the heater's
purr, though not her name.

O swallow, is it worth the loss of
such fragments to be unbroken,

to be unaware of the sibilant lettuce
issuing invitations under its own steam
in the cold frame,
                            and the way asparagus
gasps and aspires in its trenches, its purple
helmets rising again as the forays begin,
the fighting back over lost ground?

Harrier Weather

Would it head for contrail height
or hump and close and streak
crosswise down the atmosphere?
This morning you thought for a moment
you were seeing a swallow
hanging out on the edges of serious
sun-closing autumn clouds, but

that's a northern harrier,
a marsh hawk, you said with
pride of certainty, since for years
you've recognized them
by the white band at the tail base
as they skim summer dunes.

Another year on an April afternoon
you thought, That has to be
a courtship flight, the male rising
and falling in deep sine waves
along the hillsides, not as zany as
the woodcock's overture to love,
but bizarre enough.

All you know about the marsh hawk
you might have learned in a book
instead of over years on the hoof,
going shank's mare, stacking the miles.
Good man yourself. Take that first time
on Corn Hill Road one May

when that male over the marsh
let go of a furry ball you thought
at first he fumbled, until
his partner flying thirty feet

below fielded it—how many
have seen that?—and bore
it off to something she could hear
crying *me me* in the tall grass.

Stragglers

The upside-down face of Captain Kangaroo
I woke to years ago on a couch behind
unfamiliar children watching TV, my terror
that all I drank at a wedding rehearsal
the night before had scrambled
my ocular equipment. I was the straggler
then, and that was one kind of astonishment,
but these days it's more likely to be
a sparrow bedraggled by three days of rain,
a wild underhang of feathers
below its tricolor brown, black, and white,
until I notice the bird's way too hefty,
the beak's pink and wrong, and that's
not a sparrow's grab-and-go at the feeder.
It is hanging around as if lost, a blow-in
on a northeast storm who has followed
the locals to a seed source, its white eyestripe
at first perhaps a Peabody bird's,
then another kind of astonishment:
it may be a rarity from one of those islands
where puffins are a food staple
instead of a postcard. Good enough,
but just once more I wish another
memorable face were studying my sleep
through the window screen at Long Pond,
a foot away and taking me in so benignly
that ever since I've believed
St. Francis had a dog called Brother Beagle.

Survivalists

Whoever invented cursive script
must have been studying
one of those swallow-tail kites
up there.
          That September evening
they seemed larger versions
among the hunting swallows,

sharp-winged, tails deeply forked
as they twisted and rolled, picking off
insects.
          This far north they must be
a subspecies. Nevertheless
I was happily distracted from that nuthatch

drinking moisture in the rain gutter
out of a dry, cupped leaf
red as its belly.
          It had turned me away
from the chipmunks in the oaks,
agitating twigs as they plucked acorns,

all this before the sun departing
through pines made a faint, concave
rainbow in the mist cloud

above my head, a blessing so brief
when I looked up again
it was gone,
          and the nuthatch, then
the kites as though they had shrunk
to circling swallows.

The chipmunks still harvesting
were sure signs of another fruitless
winter to come,

the way they walked off
upright with my apples and Asian pears,
carrying one at a time
in their paws like potluck suppers.

Snowy Owl

Until he turned his yellow glare
on me, he was a two-foot clump of snow
in the wind-chopped flow of sand
and grasses beaten gold behind
the dunes, then a white lump
down off the taiga from Keewatin
or Ungava, part of an irruption fleeing
a crash in the lemming population,
hungry enough to risk the open
and daylight. There was little threat
here off the grid except from me,
though he didn't fly, instead leaned
at me, yellow eyes not beseeching
but weighing the moment, as though to see
if I'd phone him in to the bird club,
as if he had already somewhere
encountered a gaggle of them (one I know
took the buzzing of a wren
for rattlesnakes, and a few thought
geese calling far up the dark were wolves;
another believed the moon throws open
her celestial closet and dons on a whim
one night a sickle, a sky boat
the next), identical in their club gear,
scooting and tiptoeing, crouched,
adjusting scopes with jeweled
escarpments, checking this alien off
on their digital life lists
and heading back to the van.

A Promise

Worm-eating warbler at first,
waiting your turn after the jays
and blackbirds at the suet,
but no worm, and a cinnamon cap
instead of headstripes. Fifty years here
and as the icecaps melt
the tides grow higher and deeper
out of the North, and from
the low-country South of swamps
and river bottoms new birds migrate.

Last August a pair of swallowtail kites,
and now a Swainson's warbler, you,
rare even to ornithologists, hardly seen
north of the Chesapeake let alone here
in coastal Massachusetts, where maybe
six is the all-time count.
But here you are by Heron Pond.

As for me, I've logged Manx shearwaters
and hoopoes, wheatears, and various wagtails,
a couple of Africa-bound turnstones
on a freighter's rail, even flown
to the chachalacas and chukars.

Hunting sustenance, you skulk and shuffle
along the ground, overturning leaves,
flipping fodder, a monotype, one of a kind.
Therefore I will not turn you in for any notice
or official count. Let the flyway
that passes my door keep our secrets.

Watched Over

In the deep January nights, when the light of the Wolf Moon falls
like ringing iron through the trees, from Tom's Hill and Cathedral
Hill on either side of the marsh and Little Pamet River come the
calls of the great horned owls, those five-part queries and responses
that translate into something like "Can you hear me?" and "I can
hear you," "Are you near me?" and "I am near you." Great horned
owls go through this chthonic courtship ritual every year, and lying
deep under quilts, we can almost set the year's clock by them. In
a few months, after their offspring have fledged and left the nest,
some nights we'll hear one or the other owlet landing with a thump
on the roof over our heads. Or one day, I'll look up from turning
the soil in the potato bed or feeding compost into a tomato patch
because I just heard something say *"Schrreeep!"* and there'll be an
owlet watching me with those black pupils surrounded by bright yel-
low, the corpse-candles of folklore.

But before that can happen, the male owl—the one with the lower
voice of the two calling back and forth out there—has to bring to the
nest his courtship gifts, presentation pieces he lays on the brim of a
matted construction site the size of an automobile tire. Sometimes
it's an old hawk's nest the two owls have appropriated; other times
it's a nest they've returned to year after year, since they're monoga-
mous. The gifts consist of rabbits, skunks, cats, mice, moles, voles,
toads, frogs—you name it. As the female sits on her eggs, there's li-
able to be a heap of fur, or rather furs, hanging over the nest's edge,
though not elegantly.

For years, two owls used a nest in a pine about 150 feet from our
back door, and that meant there wouldn't be any frogs in the garden
that year and that, walking the dog, I'd occasionally find a dead rab-
bit by the side of the road, intact but for a surgical-looking slit at the
back of its head where the owl went for its brain. Owls apparently
consider brains a delicacy, and when there's plenty of food around,
they may leave the rest of the victim. Perhaps that's what the horned

owl that zipped down just above my head intended one night at dusk, before it flew off and got lost among the trees. Surprised— maybe even embarrassed—to discover there was more to me than a sparse comb-over of white hair.

Since great horned owls swallow their smaller prey whole, they have to regurgitate "owl pellets" containing the parts that won't pass through their digestive systems without doing damage. These pellets are small white packages that fit in your palm, dropped wet onto the ground from a tree branch where the owl was sitting. Sometimes there's a streak of whitewash down the side of a tree or on some leaves, indicating where one has fallen. When they are dry, they can be opened, and at least some of what the resident owl has eaten recently can be deduced from the contents. Teeth and a variety of small bones that look like parts from an old typewriter might be present. There might be a swatch of fur, even a set of bird's feet clutching the air as if still in pain.

It isn't unusual for us to get a whiff of skunk in broad daylight and begin looking for an owl in the trees because the mephitic skunk spray temporarily blinds the bird, who's out in the sun because he can't tell if it's dark or light. For years, we observed the annual courtship ritual of the owls, the occupation of the nest, and the owlets at the edge of the nest crying to their parents for food as the male and female decimated the area's small mammal population to stuff the throats of their offspring. Sibling rivalry begins early in the nest, we discovered, with the stronger of the offspring getting the most food. Usually two owlets could make out OK, but if there were three, the weakest one was usually doomed.

Fledging began when one of the little ones climbed up on the edge and fell out onto the ground. Or when the parents decided they'd had enough and nudged their offspring out. Then began a period of wandering around on the ground and learning to make short flights from branch to branch, under the eyes of one parent or another. One spring evening, I looked out the kitchen window and saw an owlet trying to get back into the nest. It was shaggy looking and had huge feet, like one of those stuffed school mascots. It would get about 10 feet from the trunk of the pine the nest was in, take a run at the tree, and continue running right up the trunk until gravity kicked in and it dropped back to the ground. It was still trying this ploy when it became too dark for me to see it anymore.

Reading My Poems of
Fifty Years Ago

Way down the railing,
wings akimbo, dipping
and rising in steps
the Navaho and Hopi
appear to have borrowed,

nuthatch screams its version
of *Gangway!* No other bird
is there, the runway's clear
to the sunflower seeds

and it looks like success.
Then panic: the threat
of its own shadow?
Self-consciousness?

It sails off into the trees,
a failure to follow through,
though you hear it in there
somewhere on a branch

talking itself back up, *OK,*
next time, next time.

Unpaved Ways to Geophany

> Murder your darlings.
> —Sir Arthur Quiller-Couch, *On the Art of Writing*

No, I have never elevated the birds
to the heights of theology,
though I will admit they discovered me
as I was looking for something
that would harness my random sense
of wonder, the way chemical formulae
never did. Color, for instance,
and texture. Flight shapes catching
the eye. Who is an anatomist
at first? Later their parts
would form litanies. I'm saying
remiges, malars, supercilia, lores.

It would always be whatever I saw
on some back road in 1965,
or an oystercatcher (1986) on
Cruit Island, Donegal, even puffins
crash landing where I sat
on the Noup of Noss, Shetland,
in '93, or boreal chickadees,
Red Bay, Labrador, twelve years later.

Come January, catch me in
the Sabine Wildlife Refuge, and first
week of May I'll impale half an orange
on a nail in my railing, so an oriole
shows up to demonstrate
that I know what *equipollent* means.
The next week I'll be where the river bends
away from Corn Hill Road. You bankers

and ward-heelers can call it an idiot's quest
because you will never get here. Poetry
and birds, trying to kill either is
a fop's game. Suggest it to Ted Hughes,
or Walter Anderson or Audubon.

Arriviste Houses

around Hopper's studio, South Truro

At night houselights in fog
trick them out like cruise ships;
by day they are structural
wonders: here a flying doran,
over there a pair of cantilevered
geagers. From a corner of the eye
you might catch them trying
to crab-climb the hill and feed
on any tidbit of the man
who worked in that common place
on the hogsback up there,
another kind of vessel, oceanic
miles of light falling through
its thirty-six north panes
without impediment. Before
the isolation that clustered
those shells of glass and sticks
together, it stood the dunes
alone, an austere cape where
he pursued "sunlight on the side
of a house." Obsession,
that dirty word: Corn Hill,
Marshall's Place, The Methodist
Church, before the personae
inventing themselves out loud
on cell phones in
the post office parking lot.

It Was Snowing
and it Was Going to Snow

There's a new complication in
that spraddle of branches just beyond
the pines, not fifty feet from this window
where I'm working a reluctant poem:
a deer, like shadow on snow, then two,
picking their way, nibbling cedar
and scrub ten feet from the clothesline.
Fifteen degrees, windless, a three-day
storm coming and they know it;
even I do, seeing a slate-colored
junco turning indigo, and four
deer now, daring a silence
that grows after the school bus
whines on through, a yellow rebuke
to this page where the poem came
close enough to show me a face
ruminating a mouthful of juniper.

A Late March Snow

There was "Dublin Paddy Shannon,"
a redundancy born Eddie Novick,
and there was Bobby Duke,
whose eye you didn't want to catch
for what flashed there. Maybe
the furnace, backpedaling
from zero, had started me
naming hometown welterweights
before dawn. When the sun topped
pines above fresh snow, it exposed
the roadside's splattered grimmage,
and in the tallest maple, as though
they had migrated to whatever
warmth it kept, one here,
one there, stars winked. Only sap,
you'll tell me, iced and sun-sparked
at the branch tips. You'll say
I ought to resurrect that fish lumper
who held Marcel Cerdan off for six rounds
one night in Montreal, but whatever
won't last the hour I won't ignore,
being one of the splendor's doxies
or doxologists, cursed
with this unstable bent to praise.

Hunters

As if tuning yourself to the oncoming
evening, you stand like death's Green Man
on Bald Hill over there, in leaf fall
and shadow of GORE-TEX from head to foot,
an arrow notched in your miracle fibre bow
that looks engineered to drive
a steel tip through an engine block.

If we seem to grow louder here
at the onset of the cold, more prone
to foot-stamping and banging around,
you should know that we're less
fearful of winter than set against you,
and tend to tramp the roads in sun colors
and waffle soles, obscuring the four-inch prints
a trophy buck's been tracking in sand.

So, before dusk last night, when the dog
and I came out and sang to our woodpile,
we startled him sweeping downhill
through the brush, then across the marsh,
crashing through brittle reeds.

You are a day late and an arrow short,
and those puffs I briefly thought
were gunsmoke: cattails he burst to seed
in passing out of sight.

Neighbor Fox

Slick calling card on the walkway,
not ropy with fur like coyote scat,
but as if to say *Don't tread on me.*
Not halfway through February
I'd seen the fox three times, first
stalking a great blue heron
that waded the river, that wielded
its bill like a pike-blade on its long neck,
that could open a fox like an egg.

Then noonish, where the river
has broken through, fox crossed the ice
long-legged that second time,
so I wondered if someone
had started in with bologna slices
again, thus its brassy coat
and the white trim around its ears.

A third morning, making notes
about it at the kitchen table,
I spotted it scratching at
the garden snow, as though something
extrasensory had begun. Deposits
here and there on the walkway
as the spring assembled
itself, and this morning at ten
fox came down among the butterfly
bushes and sipped from the garden pond
so I feared for the little bug-eyed frogs
who look up at me sometimes
from that water as if in supplication,
and might mistake this fox for the sun.

IV

Two British Tourists, Half Moon Bay

That yellow, pop-eyed crab
gesticulating on the stairs
this morning, signing *You'll pay*
for this! on the air, has had them,
man and wife, trying to tune themselves
to aquamarine all day, as the lizards do,
and trying to exchange a sparrow-colored
outlook for bananaquit
and Dr. Booby hummingbird.

Below the empty star fort weighing
like a stone cloud on the coast, another
slave-cobbled cliché, they share a pot of tea.
God is afraid to leave them in the dark, that's why
the sun will never set on them, the Irish
used to say, who have their star forts, too.

Their unease is a vervet monkey
crossing a road through cane fields,
and these villages, Joy Corner,
Elma's Hill, Rum Pie, aren't drawn
from the name book of that iron god
who sold them Calvin and decamped.

The Iniskillen Guards are gone.
The Empire has flown home to roost
on Brixton, and yet this Victorian tea room's
the Plantation. Its lizards stand in
for cavorting Nutkins,

while out of sight, the villages below
are blue and gold with Carib Beer ads,
their chattel houses proof those people

couldn't make it on their own, a country
England cobbled from two tribes
who've rubbed each other wrong forever.

The slaves of this tea party's forebears
moved earth toward heaven to hang
that fort up there. The British Navy
shifted breadfruit from one ocean
to another, transferred the slave-food
monkeys here from Africa, crossed
the mongoose from Asia, shuffling
fauna and flora to improve on nature,
and stranded their young queen on the coins.

In tonight's perpetual downtime, scored
by the treefrogs' whistling, the roosters'
hundred garrotings and resurrections,
these two will count the waves
that slam the beach like car doors
and collapsing fences, till leaf-head
clouds offshore grow morning showers
downward, trying to sink roots
in salt—ghosts of a rainforest
searching for home ground.

An Underworld Homily

Nicaragua, 1916

Green and alone and on the stumble,
I was digging shallow graves,
mozo for the undertaker in a yellow-dog
town where grass grew between cobbles
and the streets were markets for articles
that looked gleaned from the town dumps
of Christendom. I mean rags. Six nuts
for a centavo, green oranges the size
of a child's marbles, clay pots too meager
for a raindrop. Half a turnip. Jawbones
with barely a meat-rag on them. I swapped
my blisters for Señor Sosa's beans and rice
and what chickenfeed it took for my fill
of *pulque* or wine or *aguardiente*—
it means "water with teeth" and that's just
what it is—any mixture of the wild animals
to keep me off balance so I didn't have to face
in any direction to get me anywhere.
Maybe from old Sosa's daily nearness to human
conclusions he was pretty good to me,
baffled at least how a gringo could slip
so far down the ladder as to become
cheap labor in his hands. Sosa would study
my bloodshot eyes as if measuring how long,
how wide, how soon, and how deep my portion
under the earth would be. "No holes today,"
he said one morning. "You sweep the rich folks'
underworld." He led me back of the graveyard
to a door that might better have stood
in the castle wall in a Doug Fairbanks's movie.
Thick, nail-studded, it lay on the ground,
and he rattled an old key in its treasure-chest

padlock and propped the door with a stick
while I shakily lit the lantern. Down one iron
flight was a paved floor and vaulted ceiling.
Some *hacendado*'s private cellar, I hoped,
where I could liberate a little hair
of the dog behind his back. I was that low.
But the walls were like windows in
a department store, only without the glass,
and the merchandise was shriveled as though
it had been dipped in tannery vats:
each in a booth, each that tropical earth's
final joke, corpses, kept by some quality
of the soil. Poor bastards, dressed
all of them in their finery, gowns
and bemedaled uniforms fit for a ball.
Their boots were inlaid with ornamental silver.
Jeweled buckles on the elegant pumps
of the ladies were sad proof that vanity
lasts only to that final moment, though
who would deny a woman it until then?
I say women, but in their leathery
condition to determine a rich woman from
a poor man made little sense. Here and there,
tucked in the crook of an arm, a baby
in a christening gown still seemed to kick out
against its early termination. Over here
was a man as if bent under a basket
of charcoal, hair black and thick as the wig
of a soprano, but who could say now was he
only a laborer gotten up as a *hacendado*?
They all had marvelous hair, keeps growing
after your death, as you might know.
And the smell? Deathly sweet and perpetual
enough to keep me from stripping that silver

and making a run for it. Some ladies
mimicked ancient market crones, twig-arms
frozen in a haggle over a smear of goat cheese.
One gent seemed to plod along still, so I expected
a shaggy-headed burro beyond his shoulder,
except his mouth was stunned open as if
death's enormous moment had cancelled his
destination. Below each numbered booth, a name
scratched out with a stick before the clay
hardened. *Don Umberto Somebody of Somewhere. . . .*
"Rent paid until the first trumpet sounds,"
Sosa nodded where one, propped at a beam
as if at some *pulque* stand, glass yet to hand,
a *borracho* known thereabouts for his
perpetual skinful, seemed to laugh
through his gums at a quip still hanging
in the air. "Do you see the way things go?"
asked my employer, his warning that
I couldn't long continue on my ruinous path.
Was this makework sweeping underground
his way of telling me nothing I could do
would prepare me for their unfortunate state—
therefore to reward myself
while I took breath in this one?

Advice to Blow-ins

Shetland

In these islands you can see
a thousand different sheep for every
day of the year. Even on Foula
lying off there to the west under its cloud
are two-days worth, fifty
for each islander. But don't be fooled
by those wooly clouds
on firth-head fields among
the remains of Stone Age hut circles
and on sheilings
from Skaw to Isbister.

Forget white altogether. Up close
that dusky blue-gray ram over there
is colored *emsket,* a word the Old Norse
brought overseas with their flocks.
Bersugget, that ewe's motley, and *shaela,*
that other's black frost wool.

Where that lamb was stotting in place
just now, suddenly brisk to travel,
but stopped as though wondering what
that was all about, its mother's
red-brown is called *moorit.*

Though sometimes out of a gully on Noss
a black face with eyes ringed in white,
yuglet, may be studying you—
witch doctor, or as though a Norse warrior
gotten up in raunchy tassels

was serving out his karma
as a witch doctor, fated to graze
above a hoard of Pictish silver
he knows is buried there.

An Arable Bog

My grandfather knew one
when he saw one, and ditched this plot
so the vernal pools ran to his
tended beds. It's fallow now and grown
complex with its two-year
reprieve from my tiller. I study
its weeds. A breeze with
a northern edge to it is lifting
and dropping them into a green chop.
Even their names can contain
barbs, spurs, hooks,
stubborn glues, and beaks.
Sticktight and spotted henbit,
for instance, burdock, sandspur,
bristlegrass. There's catbriar,
veteran of battles, a coil of claws,
and putting out flowers among
this tangle as though they were
slumming, several foxgloves.
Folks' gloves in my grandmother's
lexicon, for the hands of the wee folk.
Once in Ballyloskey a little parched man
begged cottage-to-cottage for a ladle
of water, as she told it, and the woman
who wet his thirst became rich thereafter,
as the naysayers withered away.
The wise farmer in Ireland still won't
plow a faery rath under, nor I these
belled foxgloves for similar reasons.
Praise to the storyteller, and to
my grandfather whose strawberries
hung on for years after he'd gone,
and to the resilience of all three

and the scrappy weeds that arrived
here in ships' ballast and wool bales
and a breeze like today's,
and the flops of Bill Hollis's cows.

An Unsigned Postcard from Wellfleet

This face evolved out of the bay's conditions
as surely as boats take shape over time
from the waters they work. On a picture postcard
now, the horizon behind him nearly flatlining,

oyster bucket and rake by his hipboots,
soft hat at a tilt, almost western, it's Veenie
the clam warden, king of the flats,
hands on hips the only sign of his authority.

Was I seven last time I saw him, brought
by my older cousins to see his cows
and chickens, and relay some message
from his ancient friend our grandpa,

who lived only five minutes across
the old state road? Iconic now, a word
I'll bet he'd hate, on this postcard
he's "The Wellfleet Oysterman."

Who sent this test of memory? Almost
seventy years I've carried this face with me
through schools and jobs and the common streets,
but never saw another quite like it.

Behind the camera he's winking or squinting at,
I can even remember there'd be
a field of goldenrod this time of year.

V

Voices from the River

The visibility is zilch, like cold black coffee,
so I swim around down there till I bang
my head on a fender or hood—talk about
NFL concussions—then tie a buoy
on whatever's available,
a mirror or door handle.

᙮

Effortless, spontaneous as joy,
the birds send up their common cry.
Our keelboat has pushed off
the snags again and passed over
sunken timbers. We have resisted
the dark again, and cannot wait
for today. Out beyond us,
where pinetops dovetail with the horizon,
a whip-poor-will sings to detain the hour.

                    Who knows
this river's original name?
Tribal mapmakers drew these streams
without their bends and rapids, as though
the traveler's route was a straight line,
and the name changed with
the occupying tribe.

᙮

                         If the vehicle's
been down there long enough, sometimes
I can put my hand right through the body
like into a bag of chips. Then
the power-hose team comes out and they

blow the gunk off, or mostly, before
the tow truck can drag the car up.

I, Israel Whelan, Purveyor of Public Supplies,
bought these chips of metal and glass
you might think auto parts now
at the shops of Parker and Voigt, watchmakers.
Once these fractions were a chronometer.

Even ashore it looks so muddy a kid
in preschool maybe tried to make a car
out of play-dough, except you still can't tell
if it's a '56 DeSoto or a Hudson Terraplane.
So many down there when they lowered
the water to repair the dam it looked like
the parking lot for an underwater Walmart.

The white man gives us solid water
but shining like the sun, then shows us
our faces in it. When more come,
pale as snow and slow of thought,
clothed in animal skins unknown to us,

saying they are children of the Great Father,
and plowing the bones of our fathers,
laboring without laughter, how long before
no one will dare taste this stream,

or interpret its starlight
in the weak flicker of candles?

Who then will know the way
to the home of the Winter
Corn Spirits, or if Red Alder Creek
flows from the Wallacut River?

The Singing Water they call
Bald Head Rapids, where at the arrival
of the salmon, the woman of our tribe
with power over fish conducts her ceremony.
Each boy and girl is gifted
with a piece of the first caught.

Insurance fraud, murder, hotwired joyrides
from twenty-two states and the province
of Quebec, according to license plates. *River's*
a huge wet magnet, Hammy Snyder says,
and pries the panels and compartments
for small fish trying to make it through
winter in a car.

Saturnism it was called, and later
Painter's Colic, because the wines
and pigments they favored created
gout, fatigue, delusions sometimes,
toothlessness, depression,
cadaverousness. Water above

fifteen parts per billion
and we call it lead poisoning.

Batteries, auto repair workers, gasoline,
water pipes, even roofing materials, pottery glazes,
cosmetics, and of course paint.
Even today a housepainter who begins
espousing the irrational on a regular basis
may be diagnosed with Saturnism.

Sometimes Hammy pours
bucketfuls of hornpouts and bluegills
back into the water. But before
the fishing Trooper Lucey has to check
front and back for bodies. If he says,
We got another Swamp-thing,
the rest of us head for the trees.

Marina Stanislowska's Pencil

Gray and worn, the eraser gone,
I grabbed it to jot something down
at the dump swapshop, and brought it home,
maybe because your name was on it
in fading gilt. I expected to write
of snowy streets, seen through
branches from high above, a city
like Graz or Plovdiv, as in the paintings
of Kaspar Szlyz. The harvest moon
was coin of that realm, which perhaps
is familiar to you. The air had an edge to it
off Orion's sword, Marina, and only
the wrinkle of a scent some apple trees
were brewing, smoothed away on the night.

Are you one of those summer people
released back into a city whose dust
improves our sunsets here? The kind
who unfolds like a skit at the post office
each morning, steps from a Mercedes
black and faded as a Romanoff tuxedo
and huge as the Tsar's bathtub? Have you
gotten yourself up like a cabaret singer,
melted subway tokens for earrings?
Forgive me! I insult everyone like this,
then have to resort to writing of toads and apples.
Have you heard this peninsula
sigh with relief come September?

Already with your pencil I have visited
those trees whose apples hang
near pine cones and lie among acorns,
though all I intended was to depict the toad

who sleeps in a pocket of my clay strawberry pot.
Did you leave this stub at the dump for me, Marina,
knowing full well, as with everything,
there is more to it than meets the eye?

Having the Wrong Name

Your own world war ago, you drank
some tears and kissed some cinders,
Adolph, fighting for your name
on Worcester's vacant lots, a town
that calls to mind a sheep-cropped
shire, well-steepled, but spawned
a few tornadoes in a schoolyard
just for you, and isolations cold
as lake-effect blizzards. This house
has been pummeled and leaned on, too,
by wind and every form of water,
by those unnatural forces the Olafsen
Brothers, Inc., dull Viking hackers,
as you know. Once Joe Napolitano
sent his curses ninety feet at nine
dollars a foot from a cloud of
Parodi smoke down to our foot-valve,
his kind of water *mal occhio.* And by
raw wires hanging like fuses here
and there and over there, we knew
your brother Stan's logo. Fifty years,
and every tile you laid on counter,
wall, and floor is still in place,
as though you planted your two feet
back there in grammar school
and bristled at each *heil!*
goose-stepped around your name,
and vowed you'd set things right.

Phantom Pain

Cossack Lager, Sailor Hat, Blue Bullet Ale,
Frankenheim, whatever was drawn off
the bottom or top of a local tank
as too heavy or light to be the brand—

the beers I drank when I was young
and broke, I pour for slug bait now,
setting plastic cups around the garden.

Raccoons went through my beans last night,
raising hell, and tossed all that beer off,
then nosed and clawed
around the squashes after more.

I can see them agate-eyed with drink
out there, mumbling to each other,
letting go a holler,

finally ignoring the vegetables and heading
for the sunflower seeds
with the same bandit brains
those off-brands gave me more than once.

Therefore they are forgiven, though
I won't forgive myself the tricycle
I stole off a dark country road
sixty years ago, and tried to pedal
through a beach party fire. Phantom pain:

not the zing of a lost limb, returning,
but the memory of old horror shows, control
and dignity so gone that I still groan aloud.
So many prom dresses stepped on, so many promises.

A Gift from Montana

She would lay it carefully out on the kitchen table
as though it was a stolen European masterpiece
or saint's relic: a sheet thick as wallpaper,

shot through with colored threads,
hung with lace at the corners, as large and floral
as the legal tender of a bankrupt state.

Engraved above the famous seven stacks
of the Neversweat Mine, an eagle flew,
towing a ribbon whose script read,
Anaconda Copper, Butte, Montana.

"Your Great-uncle Owen sent me this,"
my mother would say. "He sent them to all the family.
Never tell anyone." So we were rich, and lived
in a triple-decker by design,

but hadn't that same
great-uncle sent word to his brothers
to stay in Boston, since there was even less work
out West than back across the Atlantic in Donegal?

Imagine the years and distances,
the fields of Inishowen obscured by billowing
smoke from those mine stacks lording it
over the shanties of Dublin Gulch,

and the transcontinental silences
wherein those stock certificates dwindled from legend
to the one-dollar bills our great-uncle's lawyer
sent East, making it legal
for the housekeeper to inherit the estate.

Sarcasm, one or another kind of scandal,
or did that dollar mean he feared
we'd sniff out his deathbed penury

and grumble his housekeeper into a euphemism,
and grind down the bones of his name?

Finnbarr & Co.

The American Kennel Club has announced plans to
admit border collies. Conformation standards and stud
books will be developed.
    —news item

1.
There's a roving eye in the Great Seal
on the dollar bill, Finnbarr, hovering
in the pyramid's apex. When it winks
at Debi's Petland, the Christmas shoppers
flock there from the movie at the mall,
where your kind has been high-jumping fences.

2.
After the holidays, as shelters begin to fill
with sheepdogs denied their elaborate herding games,
rug eaters and beaten chewers of furniture
will cringe behind cage wire, eyes gone yellow
and flat, unwilling to admit affection.

Blue collar in their meat and vegetable tastes,
denners in car trunks and under beds,
with the only true love money can buy
they might have made a stand between us
and the stranger, as you have done,
Finnbarr, then slept by choice in the one chair
that cries out for the dump.

3.
I can see your double, unwilling to answer
to four names, going deep into Madison
Square Garden for a chapeau he believes
with all his heart's a frisbee. So now
you and I know another reason for islands—

Mulliskay, South Uist, Wyre, Foula, Rousay,
Westray, Hoy, where the sheepwork goes on,
far from antennas, approachable only
when big seas allow.

Hamlet's Dog

> If thou wouldst have a true friend at court,
> get thee a dog.
>   —old Danish proverb

Because it never ran its emotions through
with a sword and dragged them, doublet
and hose, behind the window treatments,
or feared that reason's counselors
would tiptoe from the room, the prince
loved that dog like a brother or sister,
whatever its gender (at this late date
we can't even hazard a clue as to its name).
Who else read him like a poem,
studied his every inflection, memorized him,
and applauded his mindless humming
with such tail thumps? So that
when the poor animal shuffled off
its mortal coil there was
more than a memorable space in air
the prince kept stepping over
out of pre-Pavlovian habit, more than
the morning door he continued to open
before he caught himself and the sadness
came bounding in from Elsinore's back yard.
Its breed is immaterial now. What matters
is: his dog had taken its trust in Hamlet
out of the world. All unquestioning belief
in the prince had departed, and this was
long before the ghost and that girl
in the water and going away to school
and all the other furor that came after.

Down Escalator

If it comes to arthritis
forget the King Arthur jokes.
Heel, toe, heel, toe is safer,
call it the Penguin Walk,
but with or without it
keep off escalators, otherwise
you'll be rolling while someone
you can't see is yelling
Turn it off! and the faces
you do see, descending the next
aisle over, will be seeing you back
in ways that recall bookish
funerary reminders like
*What but design of darkness
to appall?* and *The Horror!
The Horror!* and *The poetry is in the pity.*
Forget the temptation to mumble
I'm not drunk, I'm not drunk.
You won't be able to assess
the look on the face of the woman
who hands you your glasses
either, because she's handing you
your glasses there by the black
steel-toed shoes of the airport cop.

Self-elegy: Dungallon Westerly Tending

Gone to ground, in no time at all I'm in
and out of states, cooling and steaming.
Not revenant but recombinant, right?
Along with a bumper-thudded dog
and the late Toot Nickerson, I'm
a town meeting of the air. Already
I've been dropped in pellets over
West Virginia, and tick at the same time
in graveside leaves. Migratory, I'm
a whole tribe of hunter-gatherers,
washed free in the first dense rains
of October, sailing out beyond the killing
frosts, convertible me, highballing through
the intersections, yellow light, green,
no red to stop me now, Marxist
though I claimed to be, defending Castro,
living off my old lady. At least I'm
feeling no pain. Maybe that comes after
the rising and falling? Got any Budweiser?
I always said I was two bucks worth
of star-forged particles, and now the walls
between worlds are down. *Nihil obstat,*
right? Right! Nowheresville, here I come!

Selling It

There are couples whose eyes fill with
unique futures for the infants
slung on their shoulders,
who don't want to know that one night
I dreamed a horse in this bedroom,
and found its hoofprints next morning
outside by the stairs. For them
we're obliterating the palimpsests
on these walls as though they're
the maps of our confusion,
interring under paint every scuff
and scrape until it appears
nobody ever stumbled through here.
Who wore these pirate pants
and shirts of flowers with Byronic
collars? Aside from perplexing
dumpkeepers, what's the use
of this kitchen thing now? Love,
the furniture's looking like one more
sermon against frivolity. I can lift
the heaviest of it a short way
with your help. It's what can't be
boxed and taped, our laughter and sweating
together, the handling and putting away
of everything done out of need
or a tickle of impulse. I think I can
do it all, all but the gathering of these
quickly changing faces
scattered through rooms like a game
of fifty-two pickup, their pictures
the only proof they passed through
grades and hairstyles, riding
the sine curve of sadness and happiness,
to vanish as we will somewhere out there.

After the Stroke

for the visiting nurses

It might have been as efficacious
to deposit you in the hold of a passing ship
flying the Skull and Crossbones
and hope for a cure that way
as to leave you in the hands of that crew
of insurance buccaneers, whose dialects
assured indifference if not hostility. That's how
I thought after the young doctor, cradling
his clipboard and tiny smile, announced
you'd never walk again—that sunset
on your brain's right side—and I brought
you home, convinced there was more than half
of you left after our forty years together. Was I
seeing things: after two days, tentative,
as if asking to be useful, your left leg
began its twitch. Then those VNA women
found us. "We can work with this," one said.
Gait belt, quadra cane, leg brace. She pulled
low-tech balloons and a beachball
from canvas bags, a wide yellow stretch band
to wrap your knees and make you push
against paralysis. When I think there's not
much work worth the effort anymore,
I remember how the marvelous showed up
on time in street clothes: one with a fight song
for you—though she was no cheerleader
but a slave driver showing a glimpse of the muse.
Inertia's movers and shakers, those therapists,
and one with a personal fury against No!

Ghost Flights Floating Down

Sepias of an old winter: a man standing
full height under a berg like a grotto
deposited on the beach, behind him
the marshes a frieze of no color,
spiky with terrors, a northeast wind
you can almost feel in the photo.

Months of snows off the polar cap,
with ghost flights floating down
to cut in and fuel yellow eyes
on the backs of rabbits opened and left.

All night the houses complained
around stoves, the cold beaking entry,
and the stories were of a coastguardsman
stumbling along his beach route upon
an owl untying the mysteries of a cod,

of fish sealed in the river like sequinned
slippers, as if the world's integument
had turned inside out
and warm-blooded life went on down there.

A white owl in November means weather
you'll remember, a saw new-minted that year.
When, watched by snow, a man learned
to look about him for a pair of gold eyes,
and looked beyond mud season for something
like a stump leaning sideways as if
hanging on in a gale,

and beyond the sepia crew of the *Hannah Rich*
caught waving on deck as though reprieved
of mortal duty, a joyride of breaking ice
that kept them and left for the horizon.

In the Silence of All Systems Motorless

Waiting things out, we play
Scrabble by firelight, blessedly lacking
the spokespersons of the airwaves,
with only the woodstove
snapping up oak to heat its pig iron,

that sound making me think of
Francis Chichester praising the natural fibers
like wool and hemp, and cursing out
the chemical wonders that frayed
and split in the winds of
the Roaring 40s as he rounded
the world in his *Gypsy Moth*.

Where are the experts who take
credit for halcyon weather? Another
northeaster has blown two feet
of ocean-effect snow past them,
and taken our heat and light
with it up the Gulf of Maine.

And now, as though a Blakean figure
might appear, an opening in the clouds
above the southeast hills
is edged with glimmer: three days
past full, the Snow Moon suffuses these
windless woods with a shade of blue
no sea could concoct, otherworldly,

not the sky in a children's book of Peru,
and of no weed or wing I recognize,
lighting the stripe of snowpack
down each trunk. What smiles as
that other world looks in, our house
turned chapel in the candled dark.

CPSIA information can be obtained
at www.ICGtesting.com
Printed in the USA
LVHW090238031120
670488LV00003B/283

9 780807 172216